SIMPLE WAYS TO AVOID ONLINE

BUSINESS MISTAKES

I0490747

"How to succeed in an online
business"

Jane F. Clinton

DEDICATION

I dedicate this book to my loving mother Victoria Clinton for her endless love and support.

CONTENTS

FAILING TO HANDLE YOUR ONLINE BUSINESS AS A LEGITIMATE
ENTERPRISE

The majority of individuals who launch an online business do so out of curiosity. They get a domain name and hosting and play about it since they have read a lot of exaggerated claims about how they can make a fortune with just a few mouse clicks. They adhere to the procedures provided in a training course that makes grand promises. claims of instantaneous traffic, and other BS. They quickly lose interest and give up when they realize there is no such thing as generating a fortune in their undies by utilizing "miracle software "and clicking their mouse. The fact is that starting an online business is really inexpensive. A domain costs about $10 per year. And web hosting $10 a month. If you install the WordPress blogging platform then you can

set up a website for free. So with so little invested it is no wonder that so many people give up when

they realize that it is not as easy as they think.

If you don't treat your online business as a proper business then you are much more likely to fail. You do not have to invest a lot of money but you do need to make an emotional investment in your online business.

Setting up an online business is relatively easy – making it a success is not. It doesn't matter what

Others tell you there is work involved to create a robust and sustainable online business. You will need to invest in tools like an autoresponder service to make it work properly.

You need to believe that you are creating an asset. The website that you build is your asset. Using this technique, you could earn a sizable profit by selling your website to a potential buyer. If you decide to sell your online business once it becomes profitable and popular, many people will be interested in doing so.You must work on building a successful online business every day. Forget about the miracle software bullshit. You must develop the skills to act ethically and constantly promote your online business.

Your chances of success dramatically decrease if you treat your online business as a hobby or a passing fad.

Imagine putting your entire life's money into a physical storefront in the neighborhood mall. You can accomplish that by treating your online business like a legitimate enterprise.

NOT HAVING A GOOD STRATEGY

Do you believe that many people who launch an online business have a plan for it? The response is not many. Nobody is really sure how many online firms fail each year, but it must be a large number. Most new online business owners don't have any form of plan or establish any sort of goals. When everything fails they are shocked.If you are going to start a n online business then set a goal for it. The easiest goal to set is a financial goal. Think about how much you want your online business to generate in the first 12 months and then turn that into your financial goal.You are probably starting an online business because you believe that it can provide you with the freedom that you crave. This is fine and a successful online business can provide you with freedom. No more working a dead end job and commuting for hours. Your online business has the potential to make you a lot of money. The only thing standing in the way is you. So use the SMART goal process to set your goals. Here's what it means if you're not familiar with this procedure:

Your aim must be specific; for example, "I'll generate $100,000 in revenue from my online business in the next year."

Measurable: Your objective ought to be something you can track your progress toward. Thankfully, there Obtainable; disregard the hype. You are highly unlikely to earn a million dollars in your first year of business. Realistic but not unattainable - consider the time you have available

and other resources like money
Timed- Your goal must include a deadline, like a year. Open-ended objectives are meaningless.
You must develop a strategy to reach your objective after you have set it. The end result is a daily list of chores you can complete to advance toward your objective. Therefore, consider your plan's macro tasks before breaking them down into daily micro tasks.
An easy strategy would be:
Choose your internet business model and niche.
create a website
Add material and promotions.
Promote

These are high level actions, therefore it seems sense that there will be supporting tasks to complete them. You can get started right away, for instance, by choosing the niche you want to enter. Your ideas and goals should be written down and carried with you at all times. Not having a strong brand identity can limit the recognition and appeal of the business. A strong brand identity sets the business apart from competitors and communicate it's values to customers. Neglecting to establish a strong brand can result in a lack of recognition and a failure to connect to potential customers. Not having a clear target audience can reduce the effectiveness of marketing efforts. It is essential to identify the target market for business and tailor the marketing strategy accordingly. Without a clear understanding of the audience, the business may struggle to reach and convert potential customers.

SELECTING THE WRONG NICH

You should give considerable thought to the niche you select for your online business. If you do this wrong, you could invest a lot of time, energy, and money without receiving much in return. Although there are countless niches, not all of them are suitable for an online business.

Many tips for starting an online business advise you to pursue your passions. This is done with good intentions. You will be more motivated to succeed if you launch an online business in a niche about which you are enthusiastic.If the market you are enthusiastic about has the potential to pay out handsomely, then that is all very well.

How many other individuals are going to share your love for sheep shearing in the Outback? When picking a niche, you should consider the following two factors:

Does there exist a demand?

Is the niche profitable?

It is fine if the market you are passionate about has the potential to reward you handsomely.

How many others are going to enjoy sheep shearing in the Outback as much as you do? You should take into account the following two aspects while choosing a niche:

Is there a demand?

Is the market niche lucrative?

If "no" is the answer to any of these queries, you should look into another speciality. If a specialization is in demand, you may find out using the free Google Keyword Planner. Enter a few seed keywords related to your area of expertise, such as "drone photography, "to learn how frequently people look for this and related topics. Example: Fitness and health, including weight loss

Creating wealth via earning money online,

purchasing, etc.

improved relationships, meeting boys/girls, self-improvement, etc.

Personal development

If you have any doubts about your choice of niche, follow the money. If you are currently a novice in the field,don't worry. You can get proficient in it. This is preferable to picking an incorrect specialty for which you have enthusiasm and expertise. Failing to invest in a professional website can lead to poor user experience and deter potential customers. A website is the face of the business and serves as a platform for customers to learn more about the products and services offered. Uploading wrong information, slow loading time and lack of functionality can deter customers from engaging with the business so it is always very important to choose the right niche.

SELECTING THE WRONG BUSINESS MODEL

You can select from a variety of different online business models. Here are a few instances:
• Affiliate marketing
• CPA marketing
• Selling your own products and services
• Freelance services
• Drop shipping
• Drop Servicing
• Amazon FBA
• Your own ecommerce store
• Self publishing
It is essential that you pick the internet business plan that best fits your needs. You will need to make an investment of cash to buy stock to sell if you want to start your own online business or participate in Amazon FBA. Do you have access

to this money? If not, you could borrow it, although doing so would be risky.

It will be difficult to create and market your own goods and services if you don't have a lot of free time. You can outsource product development, but doing so will cost you a significant sum of money. Do you possess a specific talent that is in demand? Here are a few consistently in-demand freelance services:

- SEO optimized content writing
- Copywriting
- Graphic design (logos etc)
- Programming
- Web design and development
- Creating mobile applications
- Search engine optimization
- Social media marketing

If you possess any of these abilities, you can sell them online and earn a respectable income. If you do this, you will need to practice discipline because your clients will want top-notch work that is completed on time.

Affiliate marketing is most likely the most straightforward online company to launch. If you don't understand, the idea is straightforward. Many product suppliers out there will provide you a commission in exchange for marketing and endorsing their goods.

Simply sign up for their affiliate network, then direct relevant visitors to the offer. You will receive a commission from the product vendor for each purchase made through your affiliate link.You can advertise both physical and digital goods. Although selling physical goods is simpler, commissions are frequently minimal. Although selling digital goods is more difficult, the commissions are typically substantially bigger.

You can look for offers to advertise through affiliate networks. If you're interested in tangible goods,

You could sign up with Amazon Associates. There are many product promos available, but they only pay out 3% to 5% in commissions. You should keep in mind that there are many internet business owners using affiliate marketing because it is so simple to get started, so you will face competition.

Do you have the most recent best-selling book playing in your head? If so, you are able to write a novel and self-publish it on websites like Amazon Kindle and Barnes and Noble. Nonfiction book authors can also publish and sell their works on self-publishing websites.

When you use drop shipping, a drop shipping firm fills all of the orders for the physical goods you offer on your website. Since you only market the things that the drop shipping company sells, you don't need to buy any inventory. You need to sell a lot of things in this business because the commissions aren't so big.

The name "drop servicing "is relatively new, although the idea is not. It's technically called service arbitrage because you buy a service cheaply from a freelancer and then charge the client more for it.

You might make a lot of money using any of these online business models. You must select the option that is appropriate for you, and adhere to it. There is a great deal to learn.

All of these many online business models won't ever give you the outcomes you're looking for.

You can select from a variety of different online business models. Here are a few instances:
• Affiliate marketing
• CPA marketing
• Selling your own products and services
• Freelance services
• Drop shipping
• Drop Servicing
• Amazon FBA
• Your own ecommerce store
• Self publishing
It is essential that you pick the internet business plan that best fits your needs. You will need to make an investment of cash to buy stock to sell if you want to start your own online business or participate in

Amazon FBA. Do you have access to this money? If not, you could borrow it, although doing so would be risky.

It will be difficult to create and market your own goods and services if you don't have a lot of free time. You can outsource product development, but doing so will cost you a significant sum of money. Do you possess a specific talent that is in demand? Here are a few consistently in-demand freelance services:

- SEO optimized content writing
- Copywriting
- Graphic design (logos etc)
- Programming
- Web design and development
- Creating mobile applications
- Search engine optimization
- Social media marketing

If you possess any of these abilities,

you can sell them online and earn a respectable income. If you do this, you will need to practice discipline because your clients will want top-notch work that is completed on time.

Affiliate marketing is most likely the most straightforward online company to launch. If you don't understand, the idea is straightforward. Many product suppliers out there will provide you a commission in exchange for marketing and endorsing their goods.

Simply sign up for their affiliate network, then direct relevant visitors to the offer. You will receive a commission from the product vendor for each purchase made through your affiliate link.You can advertise both physical and digital goods. Although selling physical goods is simpler, commissions are frequently minimal. Although selling digital goods is more difficult, the commissions are typically substantially bigger.

You can look for offers to advertise through affiliate networks. If you're interested in tangible goods,

You could sign up with Amazon Associates. There are many product promos available, but they only pay out 3% to 5% in commissions. You should keep in mind that there are many internet business owners using affiliate marketing because it is so simple to get started, so you will face competition.

Do you have the most recent best-selling book playing in your head? If so, you are able to write a novel and self-publish it on websites like Amazon Kindle and Barnes and Noble. Nonfiction book authors can also publish and sell their works on self-publishing websites.

When you use drop shipping, a drop shipping firm fills all of the orders for the physical goods you offer on your website. Since you only market the things that the drop shipping company sells, you don't need to buy any inventory. You need to sell a lot of things in this business because the commissions aren't so big.

The name "drop servicing "is relatively new, although the idea is not. It's technically called service arbitrage because you buy a service cheaply from a freelancer and then charge the client more for it.

You might make a lot of money using any of these online business models. You must select the option that is appropriate for you, and adhere to it. There is a great deal to learn.

All of these many online business models won't ever give you the outcomes you're looking for.

THE SHINY OBJECT FALLACY

There, the grass is always greener. Most likely, you are familiar with this phrase. It implies that there are other places with better chances for your online business to succeed. The "shiny object syndrome "is the name given to this.

People will tell you that you made the incorrect decision when you choose an online business model and that you should switch to another program and pay for their training to show you how to make a fortune from it.

The wealth creation niche (making money online) attracts a lot of individuals, and they are constantly being barraged with fresh, flashy things to divert them. Every day, new programs and courses in this field are released. They'll all advise you to cease what you're doing and follow their example.

No matter how alluring another offer may sound, we strongly encourage you to avoid the shiny effect. Some people keep buying these new "wonder methods "because they think the ideal solution will eventually come around.

On their hard disk, they have hundreds of courses that are collecting digital dust. Some consumers purchase these items but never use them!

On their hard disk, they have hundreds of courses that are collecting digital dust. Some consumers purchase these items but never use them! You do not want to fall into this vicious cycle. Just pay attention to what you are doing and give it your all.

We are not advocating against investing in more training for your preferred company model.

In order to make it work, you should understand everything you can about it and be willing to experiment with different approaches. However, you must resist fully shifting course because it appears like the grass is greener on the other side.

LACK OF SUFFICIENT TRAFFIC

If you had to guess why the majority of online businesses fail what would be the main reason in your opinion? Would it be a lack of interest? Lack of resources? Not having the best Internet connection? In our opinion it would not be any of these things. The answer is:

Not enough traffic! If you do not get targeted visitors to your offers then you are not going to make any money online. You can be promoting a mediocre offer and still make good money from it if you drive enough visitor traffic to it.On the other hand you can have the best offer in the world, but if you don't send enough targeted visitor traffic then you will not make many sales, if any. Traffic is the most important aspect of any online business no matter what online business model you choose.

If you are a freelancer and nobody knows about your services then your online business will fail. As an affiliate marketer if you dont drive enough traffic to the offers you are promoting then you will not make any commissions. Without good traffic to your ecommerce store you wont sell anything – and so it goes on.

Once you have set up your online business you need to spend the majority of your time promoting it. There are several ways that you can do this. If you do not want to spend money then you can do content marketing, video marketing, social media marketing and so on. If you have a little money to invest then you can use paid advertising to promote your online business. You can go for social media ads to get the word out about your business. We suggest that you go for a mixture of free promotions and paid promotions. Email marketing is a very good way of keeping in touch with potential customers and encouraging them to make a purchase. You will need to invest in an autoresponder service and build your email list but this should pay you back handsomely if you do it right.

Nothing is more important than traffic generation. No traffic means no business. So make a commitment to promote your online business all of the time. The more visitors you get the more money you are likely to make from this. It will inform you of the campaigns that are successful and point out the parts of your website that want modification. Use this information because it is priceless. A weak social media presence can limit a brand's ability to reach more people. Social media offers tremendous chances for businesses to communicate with potential clients, with over 3.6 billion users globally. Social media underuse can lead to lost chances for business expansion and client involvement.

IMPROPER TESTS AND ANALYSES

One of the most important advantages that an online business has over a conventional brick and mortar one is the ability to measure practically everything in real-time. However, a lot of internet business owners either ignore this or don't make enough use of it.

If you're curious about how many individuals visited your website last week, a service like Google Analytics can provide that information. You can also discover more about the countries from where your website visitors came and the pages they visited.Knowing how long they stayed on your website is also helpful. You want your visitors to stay as long as they can because the "bounce rate "is what is known as. If they are leaving quickly, you need to figure out why and make the necessary corrections.

You should track everything, which is something you can do. This is particularly crucial if you are paying for traffic. You can use tracking codes to find out information such as how frequently a link was Clicked.Most social media platforms today provide comprehensive analytics tools. You can use these to assess which of your posts are performing well and which are not. It should be done more of what works and less of what doesn't.You cannot manage what you cannot measure. Take advantage of the fact that you can measure the majority of things with an online business. It will inform you of the campaigns that are successful and point out the parts of your website that want modification. Use this information because it is priceless. Revenue sources should be diversified to prevent volatility and susceptibility. It might be dangerous to rely entirely on one source of income because alterations in the market or in consumer behavior may have a big influence on the company. This risk can be reduced by diversifying revenue sources, for example by providing numerous products or services or investigating partnerships.

CONCLUSION

Running an internet business involves meticulous planning and strategy in order to prevent mistakes that are frequently made but can result in failure. Their chances of success can be increased by investing in a professional website, determining the target audience, using social media, offering excellent customer service, diversifying revenue streams, selecting the appropriate niche and business plan, testing, and analysis. The most frequent errors that internet business owners make that hinder their success have been listed for your review. You must resolve not to commit these errors in the future now that you are aware of them. Your internet business's success depends on it.

ABOUT THE AUTHOR

Jane F. Clinton is an entrepreneur, an online business coach and a freelancer. The most unique part of this book is that it is written from a personal life experience.

www.ingramcontent.com/pod-product-compliance
Lightning Source LLC
Chambersburg PA
CBHW071121220526
45467CB00004B/1997